THE ACHIEVER

Unlocking the Enneagram Type 3

Asa Eccleston Kibilski

CONTENTS

DRIVEN TO SUCCEED: UNVEILING THE CORE OF THE ACHIEVER

From the moment we learn to walk, the world throws challenges at us. We conquer the wobbly steps, then tackle the playground, then navigate the social maze of school. Some of us embrace the challenge head-on, finding a thrill in accomplishment. For these driven individuals, the very act of striving becomes the fuel that propels them forward. This is the essence of the Enneagram Type 3, better known as the Achiever.

Achievers make up a significant portion of our leaders, innovators, and influencers. They are the ones whose names decorate headlines, the risk-takers, the record-breakers. Their relentless pursuit of goals shapes the very fabric of our society. Yet, their drive can also leave them grappling with questions of identity, worth, burnout, and an insatiable need to do more and be more. "The Achiever: Unlocking the Enneagram Type 3" aims to shed light on the complexities of this dynamic personality type, while helping Achievers find a more sustainable path to a meaningful life.

The Desire for Significance

At the very heart of an Achiever lies an unwavering desire to be significant, to be admired and affirmed by others. It's a yearning born not out of arrogance, but from a deeper need to feel valuable and worthy of love. This desire is their compass needle, always pointing them toward actions that promise recognition and success. While this drive fuels their extraordinary accomplishments, it can also become an Achilles' heel, with their sense of self dangerously tied up in external validation.

The Achievement Cycle

Achievers operate within an intrinsic cycle: they set ambitious goals, work tirelessly to achieve them, bask in the brief but dazzling spotlight of success, and then immediately set their sights on the next target. This relentless climb can lead to incredible feats, propelling them to the top of their fields. But this cycle can also leave Achievers feeling like Sisyphus, eternally bound to a boulder, always striving but finding fleeting fulfillment.

The Illusion of Success

The Achiever's relationship with success is fraught with contradiction. They crave it, chase it, and often attain it. Yet, the feeling of satisfaction is often short-lived. Their bar of 'enough' seems to constantly shift upward. The moment of triumph quickly loses its sheen, leaving them hungry for the next challenge and the next promise of feeling exceptional.

The Roots of the Drive

Many factors shape an individual's personality, and childhood experiences play a crucial role. Early on, Achievers may have unconsciously learned that love and attention were conditional on their accomplishments, fostering a belief that to be truly worthy, they must excel. This pattern may reinforce a core fear – the fear of failure, of being insignificant and therefore unworthy of love and acceptance. This fear can become a relentless force pushing the Achiever forward, but also leaves them at risk of burnout and an ever-present sense of insecurity.

A Journey of Discovery

This book is an invitation for Achievers to embark on a journey of self-discovery. By understanding the intricate workings of their personality, Achievers can harness their extraordinary drive while also creating space for acceptance, balance, and genuine fulfillment. While the world may see the Achiever as an archetype of success, this book promises to delve into the complexities, the hidden struggles, and ultimately provide a road map for achieving a more sustainable, fulfilling, and authentic way of being in the world.

THE TRIAD OF FEELING: UNDERSTANDING THE HEAD, HEART, AND BODY CENTERS

In the vast landscape of the Enneagram, nine interconnected personality types emerge, each offering a unique lens through which to view the world. However, these types aren't merely about our external behaviors. The Enneagram delves deeper, suggesting that we are governed by three primary centers of intelligence: the Head, the Heart, and the Body. These centers represent fundamental ways of perceiving and processing reality.

The Thinking Center: The Head

The Head Center is the realm of the mind– of logic, analysis, and strategy. It houses our rational thoughts, beliefs, and our ability to form plans and envision the future. Types 5, 6, and 7 are Head Center dominant personalities. For them, the world is primarily understood and navigated through their intellect.

The Feeling Center: The Heart

The Heart Center is our emotional compass. It's where we experience the kaleidoscope of human emotions - joy, sadness, love, anger, and everything in between. Types 2, 3, and 4 prioritize feelings as their way of connecting to themselves and the world, making them Heart Center dominant types.

The Instinctive Center: The Body

The Body Center, often referred to as the Instinctive Center, governs our gut feelings, visceral reactions, and our sense of being grounded in the physical world. Types 8, 9, and 1 primarily process information through this center, relying on their instincts and bodily sensations.

The Achiever's Dominant Center

As a Type 3, Achievers are fundamentally driven by the Head Center. Their minds are their most powerful tool. They see the world as a series of problems to solve, goals to strategize for, and obstacles to overcome. They excel at analyzing situations, developing action plans, and executing with laser-like focus. Their thinking center enables their relentless pursuit of success and allows them to adapt quickly to changing circumstances.

Lost Connection

While the Head Center offers Achievers immense power, its dominance can lead to an imbalance. Excessive reliance on their analytical abilities can create a distance between Achievers and their emotional selves (the Heart Center) and their instincts and bodily sensations (the Body Center). This disconnection can manifest subtly or overtly. Some Achievers may be aware of a vague sense of inner emptiness, a feeling as though they are merely going through the motions. Others may find themselves emotionally numb, unable to fully connect with their own feelings or the feelings of others. At the extreme end, Achievers can become completely disconnected from their bodies, neglecting their physical well-being in the relentless pursuit of their goals.

The Triad of Feeling

The term "Triad of Feeling" refers to the three core types of the Enneagram, which are fueled by emotional intelligence: Type 2 (The Helper), Type 3 (The Achiever), and Type 4 (The Individualist). It is important to note that this doesn't mean that Achievers don't have feelings; they certainly do! However, when their Head Center is in the driver's seat, those feelings may get pushed to the side under the pressure of ambition.

Restoring Balance

Achieving balance and wholeness involves recognizing the

inherent value of all three centers. This doesn't mean the Achiever should abandon their natural strength – their extraordinary analytical mind. But, integrating the wisdom of the Heart and Body Centers offers a pathway toward greater self-awareness, emotional connection, and a life that feels balanced and grounded. In the coming chapters, we'll explore how to achieve this integration, offering practical tools for Achievers to tap into the power of all their intelligence centers.

LIVING IN THE HEAD: THE ACHIEVER'S DOMINANT CENTER

The Achiever's mind is akin to a high-powered engine, ceaselessly processing data, plotting strategies, and devising pathways to success. Their Head Center, being their primary mode of operation, gives them an exceptional ability to problem-solve, visualize outcomes, and remain laser-focused on the tasks at hand. But this intense mental focus can come at a cost, creating a subtle but persistent disconnection from their inner world of emotions and bodily sensations.

The Thinker in Chief

When an Achiever encounters a situation, their mind immediately leaps into action. They begin to analyze, assessing potential risks and rewards, calculating the most efficient route towards the desired result. While others might be overwhelmed by emotion or bogged down in indecision, the Achiever possesses an uncanny ability to cut through the noise and see the core components of any challenge. This clarity of thought is a driving force behind their success.

The Strategist's Mindset

Achievers are natural strategists. Their minds are constantly mapping out possibilities, envisioning potential outcomes, and formulating plans. This mental agility allows them to pivot swiftly, seizing opportunities others would miss. They are masters of adaptation, capable of adjusting their course on the fly while never losing sight of the ultimate goal.

Focus Under Fire

Achievers are known for their exceptional ability to remain focused, even under immense pressure. Their mental clarity cuts through distractions, allowing them to compartmentalize and prioritize in high-stakes situations. This capacity to stay on track propels their success but can also lead to a neglect of other areas of their lives, including relationships, well-being, and their own emotional needs.

The Perils of Living in the Head

Despite the extraordinary strengths of their Head Center, Achievers face specific challenges arising from their mental dominance. Here are some of the consequences of neglecting the Heart and Body Centers:

- **Emotional Disconnect:** Achievers may inadvertently suppress their emotions, opting instead to process challenges through their intellect. When feelings are consistently ignored or dismissed, an inner emptiness can emerge. Difficulty connecting with others on an emotional level may also arise, as the language of the heart can feel foreign to the Achiever.

- **Lost Intuition:** The Body Center houses our gut feelings – instincts honed over millennia of human evolution. However, Achievers can become so reliant on logic and analysis that they downplay the subtle whispers of their intuition. This can lead to misjudgments or missed opportunities, as gut instincts often carry invaluable information.

- **Ignoring Bodily Needs:** In their drive to achieve, Achievers can neglect the essential needs of their physical body. Overwork, lack of sleep, and insufficient attention to health can become commonplace. Yet, our bodies are the vehicles through which we experience the world. Ignoring their signals can lead to burnout, lowered energy levels, and ultimately, compromised performance.

The Path to Greater Balance

Living predominantly in the Head Center isn't inherently negative. For Achievers, their analytical brilliance is their superpower. However, achieving true balance and fulfillment requires understanding how to leverage the strengths of their dominant center while consciously tapping into the wisdom of their Heart and Body. This integration unleashes their full potential.

The upcoming chapters will offer practical tools and exercises for Achievers to strengthen their connection with their emotional and instinctive centers. By embracing a holistic approach to self-development, Achievers can achieve not only external measures of success but also a deep sense of internal peace, grounding, and connection to themselves and those around them.

WINGS OF AMBITION: HOW 2S AND 4S INFLUENCE THE ACHIEVER

Picture the Enneagram as a wheel. At its center lie the nine core personality types. However, like feathers on a wing, two adjacent types influence each core personality. These neighboring types are known as "wings." While an individual's core type remains their primary driver, wings subtly add nuance, flavoring their personality with additional traits and tendencies.

For Achievers, the most common wings are Type 2 (The Helper) and Type 4 (The Individualist). It's important to note that no Achiever is purely their core type; wings provide additional depth and complexity. Let's delve into how each wing can shape an Achiever's perspective, behaviors, and overall experience of the world.

The Striving Two Wing (Type 3w2)

Achievers with a Type 2 wing are often incredibly charming, socially adept, and attuned to the needs of others. This wing grants them a touch of warmth and a desire for genuine connection that can soften the sometimes overly-focused drive of a pure Type 3. Their ambition is tempered by a heartfelt desire to be appreciated and liked. They are masters at networking, their natural charisma opening doors and smoothing their path to success.

However, the 3w2 Achiever may also run the risk of overextending themselves. Their drive to achieve can become intertwined with a need to be seen as helpful and indispensable. This can lead to difficulty saying "no," putting boundaries in place, and an underlying fear of rejection if they aren't perceived as worthy of love and attention.

The Individualistic Four Wing (Type 3w4)

The Type 4 wing infuses the Achiever with a streak of creativity, a yearning for self-expression, and a heightened sensitivity to their own emotional landscape. This combination can give rise to incredibly innovative and impactful individuals – those who leave their mark on the world by breaking the mold and pushing boundaries. 3w4 Achievers often possess a flair for the dramatic and an aesthetic sensibility that sets them apart.

Yet, a Type 4 wing can also bring a touch of melancholy and a tendency toward introspection. 3w4 Achievers may be prone to bouts of self-doubt or a feeling that something is missing amidst their external triumphs. Comparing themselves to others can stir up feelings of envy or an intense longing for the authentic and unique.

Understanding Your Wing

Here are some key questions to help Achievers identify their dominant wing:

- **People Focus vs. Task Focus:** Do you find yourself naturally oriented towards building relationships and ensuring others feel valued (Type 2 influence) or more focused on the task at hand, even if it means ruffling a few feathers (core Type 3)?

- **Need for Approval vs. Need for Distinction:** Does a desire to be liked and appreciated drive you as much as your ambition (Type 2 influence), or do you prioritize standing out as unique and different (Type 4 influence)?

- **Enthusiasm vs. Intensity:** Do you approach life with infectious enthusiasm, quickly moving from one project to the next (Type 2 influence), or does a depth of feeling and an introspective nature sometimes color your experience (Type 4 influence)?

Embracing Your Wings

Recognizing your dominant wing is an important step in the Achiever's journey of self-awareness. Wings are not something to overcome or change but rather aspects of your personality to understand and integrate. Each wing offers its own gifts and challenges. As Achievers become more attuned to the nuances of their wings, they gain a richer understanding of their motivations, blind spots, and potential areas of growth. Ultimately, this self-knowledge is the key to living authentically, building healthy relationships, and achieving success in a way that feels fulfilling and sustainable.

THE STRIVING TWO WING: SEEKING VALIDATION THROUGH ACHIEVEMENT

The Achiever with a dominant Two wing (3w2) navigates the world with a unique blend of ambition and a yearning for connection. Their drive for success is interwoven with a deep-seated desire to be appreciated, loved, and seen as indispensable. This combination creates individuals who excel at building relationships, winning over hearts and minds, and ultimately propelling themselves toward significant achievements.

The Heart of the Charmer

3w2 Achievers are often referred to as "The Charmer." This stems from their innate ability to connect with people, build rapport, and foster a sense of trust and admiration. Their genuine desire to help and support others, a characteristic gleaned from their Two wing, softens the sometimes-sharp edges of pure Type 3 ambition. They possess a warmth and charisma that draws people in, making them highly effective leaders, networkers, and influential figures.

The People-Pleasing Trap

While their interpersonal skills are a tremendous asset, Achievers with a Two wing must be mindful of a potential pitfall: the pervasive need for approval. Their self-worth can become dangerously intertwined with how others perceive them. This can manifest as people-pleasing behaviors, difficulty setting boundaries, and an overextension of themselves to win favor and validation. If they sense disapproval or feel their value is questioned, a deep-seated fear of rejection can be triggered, fueling insecurity and even a sense of worthlessness.

The Achievement-Love Cycle

For a 3w2 Achiever, success and love become interlinked. They may unconsciously believe that achievements are the primary way to earn affection and ensure they are worthy of love and acceptance. This can lead to a relentless pursuit of external validation and a tendency to sacrifice personal needs or desires for the sake of pleasing others or ensuring a successful outcome. Even when accolades and recognition are received, the satisfaction is often short-lived, as the underlying need for connection may not be fully addressed.

Finding Balance

The key to growth for 3w2 Achievers lies in cultivating a stronger sense of intrinsic self-worth that isn't solely dependent on external achievements. This involves recognizing that while their ambition propels them forward, they are already worthy of love and belonging simply for who they are, not just for what they do. Here are some ways to achieve this:

- **Self-Compassion:** Achievers are notoriously hard on themselves. Practicing self-compassion allows them to accept their imperfections and understand that setbacks don't equate to personal failure.

- **Focus on Relationships:** Intentionally cultivate genuine connections based on mutual respect and shared values, rather than perceived benefits to their own advancement.

- **Discernment in Helping:** Learn to differentiate between offering authentic support and overextending themselves out of a need to be liked. Set healthy boundaries and practice saying "no."

Embracing Authenticity

As 3w2 Achievers gain greater awareness of the complex interplay between their ambition and their need for validation, they become better equipped to build a more sustainable path forward. By harnessing their natural drive while simultaneously nurturing their innate need for connection, they discover true authenticity. This integration unleashes their full potential, both in their personal lives and their professional endeavors, ultimately leading to a greater sense of fulfillment beyond any external measures of success.

THE INDIVIDUALISTIC FOUR WING: STANDING OUT FROM THE CROWD

The 3w4 Achiever is a fascinating paradox. They combine the relentless drive for success characteristic of Type 3s with a streak of individuality and a yearning for self-expression that stems from their Four wing. This intriguing blend creates individuals who possess not only ambition but also a unique vision and a powerful need to leave their mark on the world.

The Creative Innovator

A Type 4 wing infuses the Achiever with a flair for creativity and a deep well of emotion. This grants them an ability to think beyond the conventional, to visualize the extraordinary. 3w4 Achievers aren't content with simply replicating previous successes; they crave the challenge of breaking new ground. Their work often carries an emotional depth and aesthetic sensibility that sets it apart, leaving a lasting impression on those who witness it.

The Quest for Authenticity

While driven by the desire to achieve, 3w4s also yearn to live life authentically. They reject the notion of blending in or adhering to standards that feel contrived. This desire for authenticity can manifest in their personal style, their chosen career path, or even in the way they choose to live. They resist the mold and push for a life that expresses their unique essence.

The Shadow Side of Sensitivity

The presence of a Four wing also introduces a touch of introspective melancholy. 3w4 Achievers are prone to comparing themselves to others, sometimes triggering bouts of envy or a sense of inadequacy. The fear of being ordinary or unremarkable can be a persistent shadow, fueling an even more intense drive for distinction. They may also grapple with a deep sense of longing - a feeling that something vital is missing despite their outward success.

The Price of Intensity

The internal landscape of a 3w4 Achiever is one of sharp contrasts and emotional intensity. While their drive and creativity propel them towards incredible achievements, it can also lead to a sense of restlessness and dissatisfaction. Prone to feeling deeply, their highs are exhilarating, but their lows can be equally consuming. If left unchecked, this intensity can lead to burnout or a sense of existential angst.

Navigating the Inner World

For 3w4 Achievers, self-awareness is key. Understanding the interplay between their ambitious nature and their sensitivity to their own emotions allows them to harness those elements in a way that's ultimately fulfilling. Here are some strategies:

- **Creative Expression:** Find healthy outlets for emotional expression, such as art, writing, or music. This can offer a place to process complex emotions, fostering greater self-understanding.

- **Embrace Imperfections:** Develop self-compassion, recognizing that everyone has flaws and vulnerabilities. This reduces the pressure to be constantly perfect, a hallmark of Achievers.

- **Prioritize Reflection:** Carve out time for introspection. Journaling, meditation, or therapy create space for processing their internal world, providing a greater sense of clarity and peace.

The Power of Integration

When 3w4 Achievers embrace both their driven nature and their sensitivity, they become a force to be reckoned with. Their creative vision, combined with their ambition and their deep yearning for authenticity, gives them the ability to create work that not only achieves tangible results but also resonates on a profound emotional level. Integrating those aspects of themselves ultimately leads to a sense of fulfillment that transcends simple external achievement.

THE MASK OF SUCCESS: IMAGE, IDENTITY, AND THE ACHIEVER'S PERSONA

If there's a skill Achievers have mastered, it's the art of crafting a successful image. From their carefully curated attire to their meticulously polished resumes, they project an aura of competence, confidence, and undeniable accomplishment. Yet, behind this facade of success often lies a complex relationship with identity and a subtle fear of being exposed as imperfect or, even worse, as a failure.

The Persona

The term "persona" stems from ancient Greek theater, where actors would don masks to portray specific characters. For Achievers, their persona is the image they present to the world – the tailored version of themselves they believe will guarantee success, admiration, and acceptance. This persona is meticulously constructed to highlight strengths, minimize weaknesses, and above all, appear exceptional.

Why the Mask?

The genesis of the Achiever's persona is multifaceted. In childhood, they may have subconsciously learned that achieving and exceeding expectations earned them positive attention and love. The fear of failure or of being seen as ordinary becomes a powerful motivator to maintain the successful image at all costs. The persona becomes a protective shield, a way to control how others perceive them, ensuring that any hint of insecurity or vulnerability remains well-hidden.

The Success Trap

While their persona can be an effective tool for navigating the professional world, it can also become a cage. Achievers can become so attached to this image that it begins to erode their true sense of identity. They may start to believe the hype, conflating their external achievements with their intrinsic self-worth. This makes them vulnerable; any perceived threat to their success, any sign of weakness, can trigger intense feelings of shame and a deep fear of being unmasked.

Living Behind the Mask

The constant pressure to uphold an image of relentless success can become exhausting. Achievers constantly monitor themselves, scrutinizing every word and action, which leads to a loss of genuine spontaneity and authenticity in their relationships. Moreover, the constant focus on achievement can lead to neglecting their emotional needs entirely. This can manifest as inner emptiness, a sense of disconnection from their true selves, or even burnout as they desperately try to maintain the facade of effortless perfection.

Unmasking Your Potential

The path towards greater authenticity and fulfillment lies in carefully peeling back the layers of the persona. This doesn't mean abandoning ambition or professionalism, but rather finding a healthier balance between image and authenticity. Here are some ways to begin this process:

- **Vulnerability is Strength:** Start by allowing cracks in your armor. Share a small struggle or a past failure with a trusted friend or colleague. The fear may be intense, but the rewards are often surprising – greater connection and acceptance, rather than ridicule.

- **Focus on Your Values:** Look beyond your job titles and accomplishments. What core values define you? How do you want to contribute to the world? Understanding your values creates an inner compass for making choices and building an authentic life.

- **Prioritize Self-Care:** Achievers often equate rest with weakness. Make time for activities that replenish your soul: meditation, time in nature, or creative hobbies. This nourishes the person behind the persona.

As Achievers loosen their attachment to their persona, they unlock a newfound freedom. By accepting themselves fully – including their flaws and imperfections – they paradoxically become more magnetic and influential. True authenticity offers a power no meticulously crafted image can ever replicate. It opens the door to genuine connection, sustainable success, and a life that aligns with their values – a feeling of accomplishment beyond any external validation.

THE FEAR OF FAILURE: THE UNDERLYING INSECURITY OF THE ACHIEVER

At the heart of the driven Achiever lies a paradox: they chase success with unwavering determination yet harbor a deep-rooted fear of failure. This fear is more than just a dislike of losing; it's an existential dread that strikes at the core of their identity and their sense of worth. It's a relentless voice whispering that any setback, any misstep, equates to the collapse of their meticulously constructed self-image and a potential loss of love and acceptance.

The Origins of Fear

Achievers aren't born with this fear – it's often a learned response. Perhaps, in their formative years, love and approval were conditional upon their accomplishments. Even subtle messages, such as parents focusing exclusively on grades and achievements rather than effort and growth, can plant this insidious seed of doubt. The child may learn subconsciously that their value hinges solely upon success, and that any hint of failure equates to being unworthy and unlovable.

The Vicious Cycle

This ingrained fear doesn't magically disappear with adulthood and success. Instead, it shapes how the Achiever approaches challenges. It drives their relentless work ethic, their obsessive attention to detail, and their tendency to overcompensate to ensure victory. Yet, the fear paradoxically increases their risk of failure. When self-worth is solely tied to achievement, mistakes aren't simply obstacles or opportunities to learn, but catastrophic threats to their very identity.

The Toll of Fear

Here's how the Achiever's fear of failure can manifest:

- **Perfectionism:** The desire to control every outcome leads to perfectionism that can be crippling. Projects may never be deemed good enough, fostering procrastination and missed deadlines.

- **Imposter Syndrome:** Despite their achievements, Achievers often wrestle with a persistent feeling that they are frauds, that their success is a fluke. Fear of being exposed as inadequate haunts them.

- **Risk Aversion:** The fear of failure can stifle innovation and bold decision-making. Achievers may stick to safe, proven paths even if they don't offer the greatest opportunities for growth and impact.

- **Burnout:** Fear drives relentless overwork, sacrificing sleep and relaxation. This unsustainable approach ultimately leads to burnout and a decline in productivity and well-being.

Overcoming Fear

Recognizing the fear of failure is the first step towards liberation. Achievers must begin to untangle the complex threads that bind their sense of worth to their achievements. Here are some powerful strategies:

- **Self-Compassion:** Achievers are notoriously harsh on themselves. Cultivating a compassionate inner voice reduces the intensity of shame and self-criticism when setbacks inevitably occur.

- **Reframing Failure:** Failure, reframed as a learning

opportunity, loses much of its sting. Every setback offers valuable lessons in perseverance and resilience.

- **Focus on Progress:** Instead of hyper-focusing on the finish line, practice celebrating progress. Acknowledge small wins along the way instead of waiting for the final, perfect outcome.

- **Embracing Vulnerability:** Allow yourself to be seen as imperfect. This fosters courage, builds stronger connections, and releases the exhausting need for constant perfection.

The Freedom of Acceptance

As Achievers chip away at their fear of failure, a greater sense of freedom emerges. They are able to take calculated risks, pursue their passions fearlessly, and embrace the vulnerability that fuels true innovation and growth. The constant striving for approval diminishes, replaced by a deep inner acceptance that they are worthy of love and respect, regardless of outcomes. This shift propels them toward a more authentic, sustainable, and ultimately fulfilling journey.

THE COMPARISON TRAP: COMPETITION AND THE ACHIEVER'S DRIVE

Achievers thrive in competitive environments. From the schoolyard to the boardroom, they are fueled by the challenge of measuring themselves against others. Competition can be a powerful motivator, driving them to push boundaries, refine their skills, and strive for excellence. However, for the Achiever, the line between healthy competition and an unhealthy obsession with comparison can become blurred, leading to anxiety, a distorted sense of self-worth, and even a decline in performance.

The Competitive Advantage

When harnessed correctly, the drive to compare can work to the Achiever's advantage. It helps them identify benchmarks of success, motivating them to reach their full potential. By studying competitors, they can refine their strategies, discover innovative approaches, and gain valuable insights. Ultimately, competition can push them to deliver work of exceptional quality, benefiting themselves and those they serve.

When Comparison Turns Toxic

The problem arises when comparison becomes the primary lens through which Achievers evaluate their self-worth. Their focus shifts from personal growth to the constant monitoring of how they stack up against others. This type of comparison fosters several destructive patterns:

- **The Never-Ending Game:** No matter how successful an Achiever becomes, there will always be someone seemingly further ahead - someone with more accolades, more recognition, or more perceived talent. This creates an endless cycle of striving, fueled by the persistent feeling of not being good enough.

- **Erosion of Self-Esteem:** When self-worth is contingent on outperforming others, inevitable setbacks trigger a downward spiral. Any perceived "loss" or instance of falling behind can severely damage an Achiever's self-esteem and confidence.

- **Envy and Resentment:** Toxic comparison breeds feelings of envy toward those deemed more successful. This can sabotage relationships and collaboration, isolating the Achiever and damaging their reputation.

- **Loss of Focus:** When Achievers obsess over others, they lose sight of their own unique path. Their energy gets spent analyzing competitors rather than honing their own strengths and pursuing their own goals.

Escaping the Comparison Trap

Freeing themselves from toxic comparison requires a shift in mindset. Here are some strategies Achievers can employ:

- **Focus on Yourself:** Shift your attention from others to your own growth. Set personal goals independent of anyone else's achievements. Celebrate your progress and acknowledge milestones, however small.

- **Recognize Your Unique Gifts:** Everyone has their own strengths and talents. Acknowledge your unique offerings and stop trying to be someone you're not. Celebrate your wins without the need to constantly measure them against others.

- **Collaboration Over Competition:** View potential rivals

as potential collaborators or mentors. Seek opportunities to learn from those you admire rather than seeing them as threats.

- **Practice Gratitude: ** Instead of focusing on what you lack, cultivate gratitude for your abilities and achievements. This fosters a more positive and abundant outlook.

The Power of Inner Focus

When Achievers break free from the cycle of obsessive comparison, they unleash their greatest potential. Their energy gets channeled into creativity, innovation, and personal growth rather than being wasted on envy and insecurity. Paradoxically, stepping away from constant comparison often leads to even greater success because their work becomes a reflection of their unique journey and strengths. By embracing the power of inner focus, Achievers not only perform better but also experience a greater sense of joy and fulfillment along the way.

BEYOND THE GOALS: FINDING FULFILLMENT BEYOND ACHIEVEMENT

Achievers are programmed for the pursuit of goals. They identify targets, strategize, and relentlessly propel themselves forward until the objective is reached. Then, after a brief pause to savor the success, they eagerly embark on the next challenge. Yet, behind the triumphs and accolades, many Achievers harbor a nagging sense of emptiness – a feeling that true fulfillment remains elusive, hovering just beyond their grasp.

The Success Treadmill

The Achiever's life can unintentionally resemble a never-ending treadmill. One goal is achieved, and before they can fully appreciate its fruits, they set their sights on another, more prestigious target. Each accomplishment provides temporary satisfaction that quickly fades, leaving them thirsty for the next challenge. This cycle, while propelling them towards external success, often leaves little space for self-reflection and the cultivation of a life that feels balanced, meaningful, and ultimately fulfilling.

What Lies Beneath the Drive

To understand why true fulfillment seems so elusive, Achievers must examine the core beliefs that fuel their relentless drive. Many unknowingly operate under the assumption that happiness and worthiness can only be reached once a certain level of success is attained. Whether it's a specific job title, financial benchmark, or level of recognition, there's always that next rung of the ladder to reach. This creates a future-oriented mindset: a belief that "once I achieve X, then I will be happy."

Beyond the External

True fulfillment isn't about reaching some arbitrary future destination or finally becoming some idealized version of yourself. It arises when you create a life that resonates with your values, allows you to experience authentic joy, and fosters deep connection with yourself and others. Here's how Achievers can shift their focus:

- **Discover Your Values:** What truly matters to you beyond achievements? Is it family, creativity, making a difference in the world? Identify your core values and let them be your compass for choices and priorities.

- **Prioritize Connection:** Invest time and energy into nurturing meaningful relationships. Achievers may thrive on competition but they are still humans who crave genuine connection, support, and love.

- **Embrace the Present:** Practice mindfulness to savor the present moment. Achievements are fleeting, but the joy of a beautiful day, a shared laugh, or a moment of inner peace is always accessible.

- **Nurture Your Passions:** What sparks your curiosity and excites you? Make space in your life for activities you love, even if they don't directly contribute to your career advancement.

- **The Power of Contribution:** Find ways to use your skills and talents to give back to your community. Helping others fosters a sense of purpose and connectedness beyond individual achievements.

Redefining Success

Achievers needn't abandon their drive and ambition. These qualities are valuable and will undoubtedly continue to serve them. However, true fulfillment arises when they learn to redefine success on their own terms. It's when their drive is balanced by self-acceptance, joy in the journey, and deep connection with themselves, loved ones, and the world around them.

The Courage to Evolve

Finding fulfillment beyond achievement is a journey, not an overnight transformation. It requires courage for Achievers to occasionally step off their relentless treadmill and practice self-inquiry: to question their ingrained beliefs about success and uncover what truly makes their heart sing. As they embrace this process, they pave their own path towards a rich and deeply rewarding life – a life where achievement is merely a part, and not the entirety, of the equation.

BUILDING AUTHENTICITY:
THE ACHIEVERS JOURNEY
TO SELF-ACCEPTANCE

At the core of every Achiever's drive is a deep-seated desire to be recognized, valued, and ultimately loved. However, their relentless pursuit of success can lead them down a path where their identity and self-worth become dangerously attached to external achievements. The persona they have carefully constructed, intended to ensure success, can ultimately become a cage, imprisoning their true essence. The path towards an authentic and fulfilling life requires embracing vulnerability and accepting all aspects of themselves, even the less-than-perfect parts.

The Armor of Perfection

Achievers strive relentlessly for perfection. This perfectionism manifests in everything from their meticulously planned schedules to their impeccably polished appearance. It's a way to control how others perceive them, ensuring that any flaws, weaknesses, or insecurities remain carefully concealed. While this desire for excellence is admirable, the constant striving for perfection can be exhausting and ultimately erode self-acceptance. When one's worth is solely dependent on being flawless, even small missteps can trigger crushing self-criticism.

The Cost of Inauthenticity

Living behind a facade of perfection comes at a high cost. It stifles genuine connection, as others sense the Achiever is not being fully transparent. The fear of vulnerability may lead to them avoiding real emotional intimacy. When they are constantly focused on maintaining their persona, they have little energy left to understand their true needs and desires. They may make choices based on how they think they "should" be, rather than living in alignment with their authentic values.

The Power of Vulnerability

Embracing vulnerability seems paradoxical for Achievers. They have been conditioned to equate vulnerability with weakness, a risk to their hard-won success. Yet, it is precisely in moments of vulnerability that they create the space for genuine connection and growth. By allowing themselves to be seen as imperfect, they shatter the illusion of perfection that isolates them from others. Paradoxically, vulnerability makes Achievers more relatable, admired, and influential.

The Journey of Acceptance

Here's how Achievers can begin the process of building authenticity:

- **Unmask Your Imperfection:** Share a struggle or a past failure with a trusted person. Observe how the sky doesn't fall. Genuine connection deepens, proving vulnerability doesn't equal weakness.

- **Practice Self-Compassion:** Challenge your inner critic with self-compassion. Recognize that everyone makes mistakes. Treat yourself with the same kindness you would extend to a dear friend.

- **Focus on Your Values:** Look beyond your job titles and accomplishments. What core values define you? How do you want to be remembered? Let your values guide your choices, aligning your actions with your authentic self.

- **Small Acts of Authenticity:** Wear something comfortable, even if it risks looking less put-together. Speak your mind during discussions even if you fear opposition. Small steps build the courage for greater openness.

- **Therapy and Support Groups:** Seeking professional support provides a safe space for examining the root of your fears and developing tools for self-acceptance.

The Freedom of Being Yourself

As Achievers loosen their grip on their polished persona, they gain access to a surprising power. The energy spent on maintaining the mask gets redirected into creative pursuits, building genuine connections, and living a life aligned with their true self. The relentless pressure to always achieve perfection diminishes. They discover that they are fundamentally worthy of love, respect, and belonging simply for who they are, not just what they do. And, paradoxically, when acceptance and authenticity take center stage, their potential for both inner and outer success flourishes beyond anything their persona could have imagined.

SUCCESS REDEFINED: FINDING BALANCE AND CONNECTION

Achievers are programmed to equate success with acquiring external markers – prestigious positions, financial achievements, public recognition. However, as explored in previous chapters, this single-minded pursuit can leave them feeling depleted, disconnected, and strangely unfulfilled despite their accomplishments. True and sustainable success requires a fundamental shift: redefining success on their own terms, with a focus on balance, well-being, and fulfilling connections.

The Burnout Factor

Achievers are at a higher risk of burnout due to their relentless work ethic, tendency to over-function, and difficulty setting boundaries. When driven solely by external goals, they can neglect their own needs – for sleep, relaxation, healthy eating, and self-care. Initially, they may operate on reserves of adrenaline and caffeine, but eventually, this unsustainable lifestyle takes its toll on their physical and mental health. Burnout leads to decreased productivity, irritability, cynicism, and ultimately a crisis of meaning and identity.

Redefining Success

Achievers need not abandon their ambition or their desire for extraordinary outcomes. However, by broadening their definition of success, they create a more sustainable and ultimately fulfilling path. Here's what this might look like:

- **Prioritize Self-Care:** Achievers often view rest and relaxation as "weakness" or wasted time. Reframing rest as essential to maintain peak performance can create a shift. Schedule time for self-care activities, and protect this time as fiercely as any major work deadline.

- **Nurture Relationships:** Connection is a fundamental human need. Focus on quality time with loved ones, practicing deep listening, and offering support. Strong relationships foster resilience during challenging times.

- **Mind-Body Connection:** Our bodies give us constant feedback. Stress manifests physically. Practices like exercise, yoga, or meditation help Achievers reconnect with their Body Center, promoting relaxation and reducing anxiety.

- **Giving Back:** Use your skills to benefit others. Mentor young professionals, volunteer, or contribute to causes that light your fire. Giving back creates a sense of purpose beyond individual achievements.

- **Celebrate Progress:** Instead of placing all focus on future goals, take time to acknowledge and celebrate milestones, however small. This develops appreciation for the journey, fosters joy, and creates sustainable motivation.

Connection: The Key to Sustainable Success

Feeling connected to others is essential for human well-being and happiness. Achievers often focus on networking for career success but neglect the deeper connections that nourish the soul. Building authentic relationships based on shared values, mutual respect, and genuine care brings a richness and depth to life that no external accolade can match. True connection makes achievements sweeter, and provides a support system through inevitable challenges.

The Power of Redefining

As Achievers embrace a broader definition of success, a sense of ease and balance permeates their lives. Their relentless drive isn't extinguished, but rather harnessed in a more sustainable way.

They learn to recognize early signs of burnout, prioritize healthy boundaries, and cultivate deeper connections with themselves and others. This shift gives them permission to experience the joy of the journey, not just the brief thrill of reaching the peak. It ultimately fuels them to make an even greater impact in the world – an impact born from authenticity, connection, and a deep sense of wholeness.

THE ACHIEVER IN RELATIONSHIPS: LOVE, INTIMACY, AND VULNERABILITY

Achievers excel at setting goals and conquering challenges in the professional realm. However, when it comes to relationships, a new set of challenges emerges. Their drive for success, perfectionism, and fear of vulnerability can create barriers to genuine intimacy and healthy connection. Yet, building fulfilling, loving relationships is essential to their journey towards balance and a truly well-lived life.

Challenges in Connecting

Here are some ways an Achiever's personality traits can inadvertently sabotage relationships:

- **Prioritizing Achievement:** Achievers often place a higher priority on their work and goals than on nurturing relationships. This can leave partners feeling neglected, undervalued, or like they always come second.

- **Emotional Disconnect:** Suppressing emotions to maintain a sense of control can create distance in relationships. Partners may sense the Achiever is holding back, leading to misunderstandings and a lack of emotional intimacy.

- **Critical Nature:** Accustomed to high standards in their professional life, Achievers can sometimes be overly critical in their personal relationships. This tendency can make partners feel unappreciated or like they can't meet expectations.

- **Difficulty Relaxing:** Achievers struggle to unwind, even outside of work. Their minds race, making it hard to be fully present with loved ones and truly connect on a deeper level.

- **Fear of Vulnerability:** The Achiever's persona is built on projecting strength and competence. Vulnerability can feel terrifying, causing them to close off emotionally or avoid discussing difficult topics.

Embracing Connection

Here's how Achievers can overcome these challenges:

- **Prioritize Quality Time:** Relationships need dedicated "work time" too. Schedule focused quality time with your partner. During this time, silence the phone and give them your undivided attention.

- **Practice Active Listening:** Truly listen to your partner, without interrupting or problem-solving. Reflect back what you hear, making them feel understood and valued.

- **Share Your Inner World:** Practice vulnerability by sharing your feelings, both positive and negative. This allows for deeper intimacy and understanding in your relationships.

- **Manage Your Expectations:** Accept that your partner is different from you. Practice letting go of the need for perfection and appreciate them for who they are.

- **Seek Support:** Therapy can provide a safe space for exploring your relationship patterns and learning healthier communication and emotional expression skills.

The Reward of Deep Connection

As Achievers become more aware of their tendencies and make

intentional efforts to prioritize connection, their relationships flourish. Vulnerability, once feared, becomes the gateway to deep and fulfilling love. They discover that the joy of shared experiences, emotional intimacy, and mutual support is a success unlike any they've achieved in their professional life.

By creating a balance between their drive for achievement and their relationships, Achievers find that their achievements become even sweeter when they have someone to celebrate them with. They discover a softer power - the power of a loving connection – that supports, nourishes, and allows their hearts to expand, complementing their drive and offering a richer, fuller life experience.

THE POWER OF VULNERABILITY: EMBRACING IMPERFECTIONS FOR GROWTH

Vulnerability – the act of revealing one's flaws, mistakes, and true feelings – seems counterintuitive to the success-driven Achiever. Yet, it's within those moments of vulnerability that they break free from the restraints of perfectionism and tap into a wellspring of personal growth, deeper connection, and ultimately, a greater capacity for both personal and professional success.

The Illusion of Invulnerability

Achievers are conditioned to maintain the persona of invincibility – they equate exposure with weakness. Mistakes are seen as potential threats to their success rather than opportunities for learning and growth. To maintain their carefully crafted image of strength, Achievers will work tirelessly to cover up any perceived flaws. This not only exhausts them but robs them of the very growth they are so relentlessly searching for.

Why Vulnerability Matters

Here's what's unlocked when Achievers embrace vulnerability:

- **Strength in Authenticity:** Paradoxically, admitting a mistake or asking for help projects true confidence. People respect those who own their shortcomings, revealing that they are committed to growth.

- **Deeper Connection:** Vulnerability is the bridge to genuine connection. Sharing our vulnerabilities invites others to do the same, fostering trust, empathy, and intimacy.

- **Innovation:** The greatest breakthroughs often arise from admitting what's not working. Vulnerability gives teams and leaders permission to experiment, take calculated risks, and uncover groundbreaking solutions.

- **Increased Resilience:** When we never acknowledge failure, we become terrified of it. Practicing vulnerability builds resilience, allowing us to bounce back from setbacks, rather than be destroyed by them.

Stepping Into the Arena

Embracing vulnerability is a practice. Here's how Achievers can begin:

- **Small Steps:** Start with a low-stakes situation. Admit to a small imperfection in a casual conversation. Notice what happens – the world doesn't collapse! Success breeds confidence.

- **Reframe Mistakes:** Failure is simply data. What didn't work? What can be done differently? When failure is seen as a learning opportunity, the sting is reduced.

- **Seek Support:** Therapists or support groups provide a non-judgmental space to practice vulnerability, build courage, and receive support to challenge ingrained fears.

- **Focus on the Positive:** Counteract inner criticism with a "what went well" mindset. Even in failures, there are valuable lessons and steps towards improved performance.

Freedom in Imperfection

As Achievers embrace vulnerability as strength, they unlock an extraordinary power. The need to uphold the persona decreases. They discover that their worth isn't tied to being perfect, allowing them to take bolder risks knowing that they'll bounce back from any challenges. They become more inspiring leaders, building trust and igniting creativity within their teams. Most of all, by finally giving themselves permission to be flawed, they forge deeper connections both personally and professionally, enriching all aspects of their life.

THE ACHIEVER'S PATH TO WHOLENESS: INTEGRATING HEAD, HEART, AND BODY

For the Achiever, life primarily happens in their Head Center. Their analytical mind, strategic thinking, and capacity to plan are truly their superpowers. However, this dominance of the Head can lead to a disconnect from the wisdom of their Heart (their emotions and connection to others) and their Body (their physical presence and gut instincts). Achieving true wholeness and living a well-rounded, fulfilling life requires bringing these three centers into a harmonious balance.

Imagine the Enneagram as a triangle with the Head, Heart, and Body Centers at each point. The Achiever, naturally drawn towards their head, must intentionally draw lines down to the other two points of the triangle – strengthening the connections. This integration unleashes their full potential. Their sharp analytical mind remains their primary strength, but it's now guided by emotional intelligence, embodied wisdom, and an intuitive connection to their own inner knowing.

The path to wholeness involves practices that cultivate presence in the Heart and Body Centers. Mindfulness meditation is a powerful tool that helps Achievers drop out of their relentless thinking and cultivate a non-judgmental awareness of their emotions and present-moment bodily sensations. Expressive activities like dance, art, or journaling tap into the creative and emotional realm of the Heart Center, allowing them to process feelings that are often neglected. Body-based practices such as yoga or martial arts foster a sense of groundedness, helping Achievers quiet their racing minds and access their intuition.

As Achievers cultivate an integrated awareness of all three

centers, remarkable shifts occur. Their decision-making expands beyond mere logic, incorporating both heartfelt values and a deeper intuition. They build stronger connections with themselves and with others, experiencing a newfound sense of inner peace. This well-roundedness fosters resilience, allowing them to face challenges with grace, creativity, and an unshakeable knowing that even during turbulent times, they can find their way back to center. Their ambition becomes tempered with wisdom, leading them to seek out work and life experiences that feel nourishing on all levels – intellectually, emotionally, and spiritually. Ultimately, the journey towards wholeness isn't a rejection of their powerful mind, but rather about embracing all parts of themselves. This allows them to live not just a successful life, but a profoundly meaningful and well-lived one.